Jesus and Me

Every Day

Eira Reeves

Book 4

CONTENTS

Gideon   Day 1—7

Jesus helps a little girl   Day 8—14

Friends   Day 15—20

Elisha   Day 21—25

Two sisters   Day 26—30

Good to work   Day 31—38

Son Solomon   Day 39—43

What's heaven like?   Day 44—48

Don't point a finger   Day 49—53

Daniel   Day 54—60

There was a time when people were scared and calling out to God for help. So God sent a special messenger to a man called Gideon because He knew that he could help his people.

Talkabout

Have you ever wanted help from God? When was that?

Prayer

Thank You, dear God, that You are always there when I need Your help. Amen

The special messenger told Gideon that he would be the one to save his people from all their trouble with their enemies.
'The Lord will be with you,' said the special messenger.
But Gideon wasn't sure about this.

Talkabout

How do you know that God is with you today?

Prayer

Thank You, dear God, that You are always with me. Amen

'Oh dear,' said Gideon, 'I'm too weak to go and fight against the enemies.'
'I'm the weakest in my family,' he continued. 'I'll never ever be strong enough to fight.'

Talkabout

Have you ever thought you weren't strong enough to do something? When?

Prayer

Dear Jesus, help me in difficult times to be strong. Amen

Gideon wanted to find out if God really wanted him to fight. So he had an idea. That night he put some sheep's wool on the ground. 'If there is dew on the wool tomorrow but the ground is dry,' he said, 'then I will know God is telling me to go and fight our enemies and that He will be with me.'

Talkabout

Have you had any good ideas lately? What were they?

Prayer

Dear God, thank You that You chose Gideon even though he wasn't sure! Amen

Judges 6 verse 38

Guess what ... next morning when Gideon looked at the sheep's wool on the ground it was very wet with dew. But there was no dew on the ground around it!
Gideon began to understand that God was speaking to him. He became much braver to fight the enemies.

Talkabout

What do you think about God speaking to Gideon this way?

Prayer

Dear God, I love it when You speak to each one of us in different ways. Thank You. Amen

So Gideon got together a big army. He gave all the men in the army trumpets and empty jars with lights in.
'We will win this battle against the enemy,' yelled Gideon, 'because God is with us.'

Talkabout Isn't it good that God made Gideon strong? How does God make you strong?

Prayer Dear God, when I feel weak please make me strong. Amen

In darkness Gideon's army attacked the enemies. 'Blow all the trumpets,' yelled Gideon, 'and break all the empty jars.' The noise was tremendous! All the enemies ran away because they were so frightened. Gideon had won the battle against the enemy.

Talkabout

What do you like about this story?

Prayer

Dear God, I love it when we think we are weak but You make us strong. Amen

Jesus was walking along by the sea. A very important man called Jairus came to Him.

'Please, please Jesus, help me,' he cried, 'my little daughter is nearly dying. Can You come and make her better?'

How do you think Jesus felt about this sad news?

Dear Jesus, You always listen when people ask for help. Thank You. Amen

Jesus began to follow Jairus to his home. On the way, some messengers arrived and they said to Jesus, 'Don't bother to go … the little girl is already dead.'
Jesus turned to Jairus, 'Don't be afraid, just believe in Me and have faith.'

Talkabout

'Faith' means believing and having trust. Talk about how you trust Jesus.

Prayer

Dear Jesus, please teach me to have faith in You always. Amen

When Jesus and Jairus arrived at the house, there was another huge crowd outside. They were all crying because they thought the little girl had died. 'Don't cry,' Jesus said to them, 'she's not dead but only sleeping.'

 If you had been in the crowd, what would you have said to Jesus?

Prayer Dear Jesus, thank You for knowing all about Jairus's daughter and what was happening to her. Amen

'Oh don't be so silly!' someone said to Jesus. 'We know that his little daughter is dead. Why bother to go into the house?' They were laughing at Jesus.
'She's dead,' said someone else in the crowd.

What do you feel about people laughing at Jesus?

Dear Jesus, it makes me sad that people laughed at You. Help me to believe You always. Amen

Even though the crowd laughed at Him, Jesus went into the house with Jairus and his wife. Jesus walked over to where the little girl was lying down. He gently held her hand.

Talkabout

What do you like about what Jesus did?

Prayer

Thank You, dear Jesus, You were so gentle with this little girl. Thank You for being so gentle with me too. Amen

Jesus looked
at the little girl who was
lying very still and didn't
seem to be alive at all.
'Little girl,' said Jesus, 'get up!'
As soon as Jesus spoke, the little girl opened her eyes!

How do you think the little girl's mummy and
daddy felt when they saw this happen?

Dear Jesus, thank You for healing the little
girl. Amen

The little girl stood up. Her mummy and daddy came over to her and hugged her. They were so excited to see their daughter alive again.

'Please,' said Jesus, 'give her something to eat.'

 What do you like about this story? Why?

Prayer Dear Jesus, thank You that You love to surprise us when You do miracles. Amen

Kim gave David a big push. It wasn't very nice of Kim to do this.
'Jesus still wants me to love you, Kim,' cried David, 'even though you've been horrible to me!'
Kim was then so sorry that he had pushed David.

Talkabout

Has something like this ever happened to you?
Did you find it hard to still love your friend?

Prayer

Dear Jesus, thank You for teaching us to love our friends always. Amen

'Do you know,' said Sarah to Sue, 'there's something very special about Jesus.'
'What is that?' asked Sue.
'He wants us all to be His friends!'
Sarah and Sue hugged one another.

Talkabout

How do you feel being called a friend of Jesus? What would you like to do for Him as a friend?

Prayer

Thank You, Jesus, that we are all Your friends. Amen

Max's special friend was Ben. They loved to play together. 'Whatever happens,' said Max to Ben, 'I hope we'll be friends for ever and ever.'
They went on playing with their cars.

Who do you like to play with? Why?

Thank You, dear Jesus, that You give us special friends. Amen

Everyone was in the kitchen eating cake.
'Can we always be friends,' said Sue, 'and help one another every day?'
They all nodded their heads.
'Yes,' said Kelly, 'we shall be friends forever.'

Talkabout Who would you always like to be friends with? Why?

Prayer Dear Jesus, help me to be a good friend. Amen

David had been arguing with Kim.
'Go and say sorry to Kim,' said Mummy to David. But David didn't want to say sorry.
'Say sorry,' repeated Mummy. After a while David knew that it was the right thing to do.
'Sorry,' said David to Kim, 'I didn't mean to argue with you. I do love you as my friend.'

Talkabout
Have you ever had to say sorry to a friend?
What was it for?

Prayer
Dear Jesus, help me to love my friends – even though we have arguments. Amen

Sue was crying because she had broken her favourite toy.
'I really loved that doll,' sobbed Sue.
Kelly put her arm around Sue. 'Never mind,' she said, 'you're my special friend and you can have my favourite doll.'

 **Talkabout**   Would you give your favourite toy away? Who would you give it to?

 **Prayer**   Dear Jesus, thank You that You teach us to be kind to our friends. Amen

2 Kings 4 verse 1

Elisha was a man of God. One day he was walking through a village when a woman cried out. 'I have no money,' she sobbed, 'and people are coming to take away my two sons.'

Talkabout

'A man of God' like Elisha is somebody who is very close to God. Would you like to be a person like that? Why?

Prayer

Dear God, help me to stay very close to You. Amen

'How can I help you?' asked Elisha. 'What food do you have in your house?' The woman went inside and brought out a bottle which had in it just a few drops of oil for cooking. 'This is all I have left,' she cried.
All she wanted was food to feed her two sons.

Talkabout Say what you are thankful for in your home.

Prayer Dear God, thank You for giving us everything in our home. Amen

Then Elisha said a very strange thing to the woman.
'Go to all your neighbours,' he said, 'and ask them to give you all their empty jars. When you have collected them take the jars back to your house.'

 **Talkabout**
What do you think the woman thought of Elisha's idea?

Prayer
Thank You, dear God, that You knew what the jars were for! Amen

'Now,' said Elisha to the poor woman, 'pour a little of the oil you have into each jar.'
The woman began to pour a drop of oil into each jar. As she did this the jars became full up with oil. What a miracle!

Talkabout

Now what do you think the woman thought of Elisha's idea?

Prayer

Thank You, God, for helping this poor woman. Amen

'Go now,' said Elisha to the woman, 'and sell all the full-up jars of oil. When you have done this you will have enough money to buy food.'
The woman was so excited and happy – and so were her two sons!

Talkabout

Why were her two sons happy? (Look at Day 21.)

Prayer

Thank You, God, for solving the problem of no money and no food for this poor woman and her two sons. Amen

In a village called Bethany lived two sisters. Their names were Martha and Mary. One day Jesus came to visit them. 'Welcome,' they said, 'we're so happy that You have come to our home.'

Talkabout

Do you have a sister? Do you have friends who have sisters? What are their names?

Prayer

Thank You, dear Jesus, for sisters (and brothers!) everywhere. Please help them to be good sisters and brothers. Amen

Martha got very busy in the kitchen. She wanted to make Jesus a wonderful meal. So she rushed around the kitchen collecting pots and pans and preparing the food. She became so busy as she cooked the meal.

Talkabout

What do you like to do when you are busy?

Prayer

Dear Jesus, thank You that You are with us even when we are busy. Amen

Meanwhile Mary peacefully sat at the feet of Jesus. She wanted to hear everything that Jesus said. She sat very still and looked up at Jesus as He spoke. There was so much peace in the room.

Talkabout

Do you like sitting still? What's good about being quiet and sitting still?

Prayer

Dear Jesus, thank You that Mary enjoyed sitting still and listening to You. Amen

All of a sudden Martha appeared in the doorway. She was looking angry.
'Jesus,' she said very loudly, 'please tell my sister Mary to come and help me prepare the meal in the kitchen!'

Talkabout

Have you ever got angry? What happened?

Prayer

Please, dear Jesus, help me when I get angry. Amen

'Martha, Martha,' said Jesus very kindly, 'please don't worry about being busy and working. Come here and join us and listen to what I have to say. This is more important at the moment.'

Talkabout

How do you think Martha felt? What is important to you today?

Prayer

Dear Jesus, help me to always find time to listen to what You have to say. Amen

Max and Sue were looking out of the window one night. 'Isn't it wonderful,' said Max, 'that God worked so hard making all those stars and the moon?' 'Yes,' replied Sue, 'isn't God's work great!'

Talkabout

What do you like about all the things God has made?

Prayer

Dear God, thank You for all the things You have made in the world for us to enjoy. Amen

'Do you know what I like best about God's work?' said Kelly to Kim her brother.
'What?' replied Kim.

'He made you!' said Kelly smiling.

Talkabout — Why do you think God made you? What is so special about you?

Prayer — Dear God, thank You that You made all of us and that we are all special to You. Amen

'Oh dear!' said David's mummy, 'I really must clean this floor. I think someone must have walked over it with muddy boots.' 'Don't worry, Mummy,' said David, 'I'll clean it for you.'

Talkabout

What work do you like to do around the house? Why?

Prayer

Dear Jesus, help me to be a help in the house. Amen

2 Corinthians 9 verse 8

Sue's grandma couldn't garden anymore. She found it all too much hard work.
'Never mind, Grandma,' said Sue, 'I'll do some for you.'
So Grandma gave her a little trowel and Sue got busy doing some weeding.

Talkabout

Have you helped someone who is elderly? What did you do for them?

Prayer

Dear Jesus, please make me helpful when someone needs help. Amen

'I really haven't got time to clean that table,' said Ben's mummy who was very busy.
'Let me do it for you,' said Ben. 'I like cleaning.'
So Mummy gave him a cloth and some cleaner and Ben happily wiped the table.

Talkabout What makes you happy when you help someone?

Prayer Dear Jesus, thank You that it makes You happy when we help others. Amen

It was Saturday morning and Max's daddy decided to clean the car.
'Can I help you?' asked Max.
'Thank you, Max,' said Daddy. 'Jesus would be very pleased with you – and so am I!'

Talkabout

What work do you do that pleases Jesus?

Prayer

Thank You, dear Jesus, for times when we can happily help with work. Amen

Sue and her mummy went out shopping.
'We have a very big shopping list,' said Mummy.
When they got to the checkout at the supermarket, Sue helped pack all the food into the bags.
Her mummy was very pleased with Sue for helping.

Talkabout

What do you like about shopping?
How do you like helping?

Prayer

Thank You, dear Jesus, that we can help when we are out shopping.
Amen

Sarah was looking at all the flowers in the garden. 'God must have been very busy,' she said, 'when He made all of these.' 'Yes, I expect He was,' replied Daddy, 'but when He had made everything in the world, He took a rest.'

Talkabout

Do you think God deserved a rest after all He had made in the world?

Prayer

Dear God, thank You for all Your wonderful work. I'm so glad You were able to take a rest afterwards. Amen

When he was old, King David called for his son Solomon to give him some good advice for his life as king.
Solomon later wrote a book called Proverbs, full of good advice for his own son.

 'Advice' means being told how to be sensible and do the right thing. Have you ever been given some good advice? What was it?

 Dear Jesus, help me to listen when someone gives me good advice. Amen

Listen to me

Proverbs 3 verses 5–6

'Listen, son,' said King David to his son Solomon, 'always walk with God and always keep His rules wherever you go.' Solomon listened to what his father was saying because he knew it was very important.

 **Talkabout** When was the last time you were told something important?

Prayer Dear God, help me to talk to you when I don't know what to do. Amen

'Another bit of advice,' said King David to his son Solomon, 'is that I want you to have wisdom all your life and show kindness to people.'
Again Solomon listened to his father very carefully.

Do you listen carefully to what you are told?

Prayer

Dear God, thank You that You can help me to be kind to people. Amen

King David continued giving good advice to his son.
'It's important to let people eat with you at your table,' said
King David to his son Solomon, 'and always give them respect.'
Solomon listened to his father.

Who would you like to invite for a meal?

Thank You, dear Jesus, for all you have given
me. Help me to share with others. Amen

It wasn't long afterwards that King David died and his son Solomon became the new king of Israel!
Solomon was so thankful that his father had given him such good and wise advice, but he also asked God for extra wisdom.

Talkabout

Who are you thankful to for giving you good advice? What was it?

Prayer

Dear God, thank You for .... Help me to do what they say. Amen

WHAT'S HEAVEN LIKE?

Matthew 13 verse 31

Day **44**
Small seeds

Jesus loved to tell stories. One day He wanted the crowd of people to know what heaven is like. 'There was a man,' He said to them, 'and he had a mustard seed. This seed was so very, very small.'

Have you ever had a packet of seeds? What kind of seeds were they?

Prayer

Dear Jesus, I love it when You want to tell us a story. Thank You. Amen

The man dug a little hole and popped the seed into it. He covered it with soil and then waited for the seed to grow. Not long afterwards a green shoot appeared.

Talkabout

Have you ever planted seeds? What did you do after planting them?

Prayer

Thank You, God, that we can plant seeds, water them and watch them grow. Amen

The man became very excited watching the plant grow.
It grew and grew and grew out of the ground. Very slowly it became a very big tree. It was HUGE!

Talkabout

Have you ever watched seeds grow? Did they take a long time?

Prayer

Dear God, thank You for all the seeds You have given us. Amen

The tree was SO huge that all the birds began to fly and find shelter in the branches. All types, shapes and colour of bird flew through the air and nested in the tree.

Talkabout

What do you like about birds?

Prayer

Dear Jesus, thank You for birds everywhere and thank You for their beautiful singing. Amen

'So,' said Jesus to the crowd, 'that is what heaven is like. Heaven is like this BIG, BIG tree that gives everyone protection and we can all be safe there.'
The crowd were so amazed at His teaching.

 Talkabout

What else do you think heaven will be like?

 **Prayer**

Thank You, dear Jesus, that You are there in heaven with God the Father. Amen

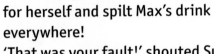

It's all your fault!

Sue and Max were eating their supper.
'This is delicious,' said Max, eating his sandwich. Then Sue
reached right across Max to pour a drink
for herself and spilt Max's drink
everywhere!
'That was your fault!' shouted Sue
to Max.

Talkabout

What should Sue have said to Max?

Prayer

Dear Jesus, help me to say sorry when I do
something wrong. Amen

David had been eating biscuits from a box.
'Who,' said Mummy, 'has left this box of biscuits on the floor?'
Immediately David pointed a finger at Sarah.
'She did!' he said.

 Talkabout

What should David have said to his mummy?

Prayer

Dear Jesus, help me, when it's my fault, to own up. Amen

Philippians 2 verse 14

Ben and Kelly were playing in the sand. They were building sandcastles.
Kelly had built a beautiful castle. Ben tried to build one but his castle fell down.
'Look what you've done – you've knocked my castle down!' he cried.

Why was it wrong for Ben to blame Kelly?

Prayer

Please help me Jesus, never to blame someone else when it's not their fault. Amen

Sarah and Kelly were sitting together talking. Then Kim came into the room.

'Look,' whispered Kelly to Sarah, 'Kim's got different coloured socks on.'

They both giggled at him. 'Doesn't he look funny!' said Kelly.

Talkabout

It wasn't very nice of Kelly to say that. What should she have done?

Prayer

Please, Jesus, don't let me laugh at other people's mistakes. Amen

Ephesians 4 verses 31–32

Don't be unkind

Sue was wearing a brand-new dress. 'Isn't that pretty,' said Kelly. Sue was very happy that Kelly had said that.
'I don't like the colour of that dress,' said David, 'it looks horrible.' David made Sue feel very unhappy.

 What was wrong with David saying that to Sue?

Prayer Dear Jesus, help me not to say things that make people unhappy. Amen

Daniel lived in Jerusalem. One day, a foreign king called
Nebuchadnezzar captured Daniel and some others and took
them to his land called Babylon. He wasn't a kind king.

Talkabout

Can you say what it must have been like to
have been captured?

Thank You, God, that even though Daniel was
captured You were with him. Amen

Daniel 1 verse 4

Clever young men

King Nebuchadnezzar was looking for clever young men to be trained in his palace. So he called Daniel and three of his friends. 'They are all very clever, healthy and wise,' said the king.

Talkabout How do you think you can become clever, healthy and wise?

Prayer Dear God, thank You for Daniel and his friends. Amen

In the palace all the king's people were given a lot of rich food. There was masses of it!
'I'm training them,' said the king, 'to serve me in the palace. That's why they must have large amounts of rich food and drink.'

Do you know what food is good for you and what is bad?

Dear God, help me to eat well and wisely so that I can be healthy for You. Amen

Only vegetables

'It's not right,' said Daniel to his friends, 'we mustn't eat all this rich food that the king is giving to us – it's against God's rules to eat the food of this foreign king.'
So Daniel and his friends spoke amongst themselves and decided they could only eat vegetables while they were serving the king.

What vegetables do you like? Why?

Thank You, God, You want us to enjoy all the vegetables that You have made for us. Amen

'Please give us only vegetables and water for ten days,' said Daniel to a servant, 'then see if we are more healthy than all the others in this palace who have eaten too much of the wrong food.'

Talkabout

What is your favourite meal? Why?

Prayer

Dear God, thank You that Daniel obeyed You and only ate the food You told him to. Amen

After ten days of eating the right food Daniel and his friends looked so healthy. They were more healthy than all the servants in the palace who had eaten the king's rich food! God had given Daniel and his friends a lot of wisdom.

Do you eat food that is good for you?

Please, dear God, help me to eat the right food. Amen

'Bring me Daniel and his friends. I want to see them!' ordered King Nebuchadnezzar.

The king looked at Daniel and his friends, 'Why,' he said, 'you all look SO healthy and well!'

The king was so amazed and gave Daniel the best job in the palace.

Talkabout

What do you like about this story of Daniel?

Prayer

Help me, God, to do what You ask me to do.
Amen

Three more beautifully illustrated daily devotionals by Eira Reeves, for 3- to 6-year-olds:

£5.99 each

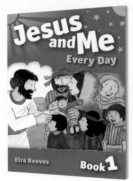

ISBN: 978-1-85345-518-6

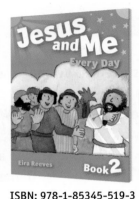

ISBN: 978-1-85345-519-3

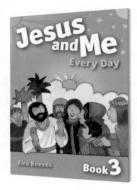

ISBN: 978-1-85345-544-5

For when you're too old for Jesus and Me Every Day

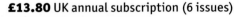

Topz helps 7- to 11-year-olds get to know God and His Word through an exciting, day-by-day look at the Bible. Daily Bible readings and simple prayers are augmented by readers' contributions along with fun and colourful word games, puzzles and cartoons.

£13.80 UK annual subscription (6 issues)
Individual copies also available: £2.49 each
72-page, full-colour booklet, 210x148mm, published bimonthly
ISSN: 0967-1307

Visit **www.cwr.org.uk** or call **01252 784710**
Prices correct at time of printing.